Private

Realities:

Recent

American

Photography

Emmet Gowin

Cary Wasserman

Jerry Uelsmann

John Benson

Linda Connor

David Batchelder

Leslie Krims

Judy Dater

Benno Friedman

Kelly Wise

Private

Realities:

Recent

American

Photography

Distributed by

New York Graphic Society

Greenwich, Connecticut

Museum of Fine Arts

Boston

Copyright 1974. All rights reserved.
Museum of Fine Arts
Boston, Massachusetts
Library of Congress catalog card no. 73—90126
ISBN 0—87846—077—2
Typeset in IBM Univers by Jane Deland
Printed by Scroll Press, Danbury, Conn.
Designed by Carl Zahn

This project is supported by a grant from
the National Endowment for the Arts,
a Federal Agency.

Cover:
JERRY UELSMANN
Diptych, 1972

Preface

"Private Realities," the first major exhibition of contemporary photography organized by the Museum of Fine Arts, marks another stage in the development of the museum's interest in photography as an art form.

The Museum of Fine Arts was one of the first American art museums to collect fine photographs. In 1924, through the initiative of the Keeper of Indian Art, Ananda K. Coomaraswamy, the museum acquired as a gift of the artist twenty-seven photographs by Alfred Stieglitz. In the years following the collection continued to grow by gift. The most notable additions were a fine group of daguerreotypes by the Boston firm of Southworth and Hawes from Edward Southworth Hawes and a second group of Stieglitz photographs from Georgia O'Keeffe. In 1967 the first purchases of photographs were made and further gifts were solicited from interested donors. Recently, grants of purchase money from the Polaroid Foundation have made possible an expanded acquisition program. "Private Realities: Recent American Photography" represents the museum's new commitment to contemporary photography as well as to the photographic classics of the past.

I would like to take this opportunity to thank all those who have contributed so generously to this part of the museum's collection and particularly to thank Clifford Ackley of the Department of Prints and Drawings for his enthusiasm and sustained interest in photography as an important aspect of the museum's program.

MERRILL C. RUEPPEL
Director

Foreword

The idea for this exhibition was conceived by Kelly Wise. Originally planning to stage it elsewhere, he was persuaded by Cary Wasserman that the Museum of Fine Arts might be interested. This was a happy coincidence, because at the time they approached me I was seeking a photography exhibition that would be contemporary and wholly different in point of view from the major loan shows that the museum had borrowed in the recent past: "Ansel Adams" (1967), "Walker Evans" (1971), "French Primitive Photography" (1972), and "Paul Strand" (1972).

Kelly Wise and Cary Wasserman served as advisors to the exhibition until the photographers to be invited had been selected. It was agreed that I would serve as curator for the exhibition, being responsible for the final selection of the images, the catalogue, and the installation. Each of the ten invited photographers was asked to submit twenty-five images, from which I selected a final twelve or thirteen.

During the preparation of the exhibition Eleanor Sayre, curator, and the entire staff of the Department of Prints and Drawings provided constant support. Linda Thomas, registrar of the museum, and her staff have proved most helpful.

I would like to thank Carl Zahn, editor-in-chief, the staff of the museum Office of Publications, and Jack Leether and his staff at Scroll Press for their enthusiastic dedication to the catalogue project.

Discussions with the photographers, with Harold Jones and Irene Borger of the Light Gallery, New York, and with Lee Witkin of the Witkin Gallery, New York, facilitated the writing of the introductory essay. The selected biographies and bibliographies were compiled and edited by Odette M. Appel, curatorial assistant in the Department of Prints and Drawings, on the basis of information submitted by the photographers. I have also benefited enormously from her organizational abilities, ideas, and suggestions throughout the preparation of the exhibition. Most of all,

however, I am indebted to the photographers who created the images that make up this exhibition.

CLIFFORD S. ACKLEY
Assistant Curator
Department of Prints and Drawings

Private Realities

by Clifford S. Ackley

The title "Private Realities" was chosen to
indicate that, although all of the works in this
exhibition make use of objective camera realism,
they are primarily concerned with the recording
of subjective states of feeling. These works are
not so much documentary as surreal, fantastic,
autobiographical, profoundly personal. The
photographers selected are only ten from among
a great number of younger American photographers working in these directions in the last
decade.

Many of these images represent a conscious
divergence from the purist and documentary
traditions that crystallized in the 1920's and
30's and which emphasized direct, non-manipu-
lative recording of the external world.

It is interesting that many recent American
realist painters have discovered and made use
of the objective recording side of photography
at a time when many photographers like those
in the exhibition have been using the photographic medium for highly subjective and personal, even literary, statements.

The photographers exhibited here have no
inhibitions about rearranging reality for the
camera or manipulating the negative or print,
so long as the desired expression is achieved.

Emmet Gowin

Cary Wasserman

Jerry Uelsmann

Emmet Gowin often uses his family and relatives as models. They are, however, posed and recorded in such a way that the individual is made to represent broader aspects of human experience or the natural world. His niece, Nancy Wells, is seen, eyes closed, arms entwined, hands clutching eggs, emblems of fertility, as if in a state of seizure or trance (no. 6, plate III). Nancy is seen again reclining, eyes closed as if dreaming, her dolls clustered about her like previsions of motherhood (no. 9). His wife, Edith, viewed through a wreath of leaves, standing within the circle of another wreath, a garland of wild berries hanging between her bare breasts, seems to be a nature goddess (no. 11, plate IV).

The latter image is contained within a dark circle created by means of an intentional disproportion of lens and camera: the use of a lens appropriate for a 4 x 5 camera on an 8 x 10 camera causes the whole circle of the lens to be recorded. The resulting diffuse dark circle creates distance between viewer and subject: it functions as a kind of time tunnel or mysterious porthole offering glimpses into another world.

The edges of the lens introduce subtle distortions and stretching of space. In *Edith with Wild Berry Necklace* the effect is almost that of an image in a crystal globe. In the recent photograph of the *Isle of Skye* (no. 2, plate I) the circular format and lens distortions help to create ambiguity as to scale: stacks of peat look like so many Stonehenges multiplied to infinity. Sometimes the edges of the circle are clearly defined; in other instances there is a gradual merging with the surrounding darkness, as in the image of the glimmering, melting *Ice Fish* (no. 5, plate II). Much of the impact of Gowin's images derives, in fact, from an intensified recording of the drama of light and shadow. This drama is enhanced by the richly modulated tonalities of the photographic print itself.

Color is usually considered an element that heightens photographic realism. Cary Wasserman employs color to transform or transcend reality. The precisely recorded rocks of Magnolia, Massachusetts, seem to glow with unearthly colors (nos. 21—24, plate VIII).

Color is only one of the means of transformation the photographer employs. In the two versions of *Elysian Fields* (nos. 19 and 20, plate VII) solarization as well as color is used to dematerialize forms and translate the rocks and the photographer's friends to a more heavenly plane. In the solarization process the negative or print is re-exposed to light during development, resulting in a partial or complete reversal of values. The circles of light created by masking the print surface with circular objects during the printing are a recurring feature of Wasserman's work. Here they take on the traditional meaning of a halo or aureole indicating divinity.

In other instances, such as the image of friends assembled at a birthday party (no. 18), the circles function as spotlights or focal points that give greater or lesser importance to the faces of the guests. One party-goer's head has been completely removed from our attention and replaced by a blank white circle. In images like the present one, these circles also create an ambiguous sense of layered depth. Another creative use of masking during printing is seen in the miraculous white light that falls from the cupola of the *Tomb* (no. 13, plate V) onto the flowers below.

The peculiar transparent brilliance of Cary Wasserman's colors could not be achieved in any medium other than color photography.

Jerry Uelsmann takes advantage of the "realness" of photographic images in order to convince us of the reality of dreams, miracles, and allegories. Working with a "sandwich" of negatives in his enlarger, he fuses the disparate images into one seamless photographic image.

One of Uelsmann's constant themes is the absolute identification of woman and feminine fertility with nature as a whole. The nude figure of a woman, curled up like a fetus, is the pivot of a landscape that explodes with light and churns with the swirling energy of moving water (no. 26, plate IX). Are we witnessing nature giving birth or a return to the womb of nature? Uelsmann's richly metaphorical imagery permits of many interpretations.

In the *Diptych* (nos. 27 and 28, cover) the two feminine figures seem to personify heaven and earth, light and darkness. The titles *Diptych* and *Triptych* (nos. 30-32) refer, of course, to the formats of Western altarpiece paintings. A traditional diptych would, however, read left and right rather than vertically. The *Triptych* with its images of fertility is traditional enough in format to include a lower narrative zone like the predella panels of an altarpiece. The aged figure that paces through this zone seems emblematic of human transience.

When divided vertically at center, both portions of the *Diptych* reveal a Rorschach blot duplication of the landscape image left and right, a paradox that frequently occurs in Uelsmann's work. Another example of such doubling of the image is the landscape in number 29 (plate X). It is also interesting that the two trees hovering above the landscape, although differing in value, are completely identical in detail. There is a science fiction feeling about this image, the invasion of a perfect Sierra Club landscape by alien plant forms. A certain quirky humor is a familiar aspect of Uelsmann's work.

The human hand is a recurrent image. In *Questioning Moment* (no. 35) a giant hand threatens the figure that cowers in the corner while, in a lower zone composed of a separate print, disembodied hands come together and clench as if in affirmation. A man's hand tenderly cradles the body of a woman (no. 37,

John Benson   # Linda Connor

plate XII). Hand, woman, the open pod form identified with her body, and the oval format meld together in one indivisible metaphor. The effect of this image is heightened by the suggestion of warm flesh tones that the print color gives. Clasped stone hands are part of the imagery of number 36 (plate XI). This is one of a group of recent works in which the images are no longer inextricably fused but are placed side by side as on a sketchbook page.

The John Benson images were not created with a conventional camera but with a 3M color-in-color copying machine. This machine includes a panel that is intended for color correction but that can be used by an artist like Benson for expressive color variations. He also recopies images in order to further transform them. The subject matter, whether living models, X-rays, negatives, or old photographs, is arranged directly on the screen of the copier to create the image. The prints, which are essentially unique, since no two prints from the copier are exactly alike in color, have been laminated in clear plastic to stabilize the color.

All of these images essentially involve a collage approach, taking found materials, two-dimensional or three-dimensional, and placing them in new expressive relationships. The collage concept (from the French *coller*: to glue, to paste) originated with the Cubist painters Braque and Picasso in 1912. In the 1920's and 30's the collage idea was expanded by other artists' use of photomechanical and photographic materials.

The images in the exhibition may be divided into two groups: those involving "body-collage" using living models and those that are arrangements of two-dimensional transparent or opaque photographic materials. The body-collage images with their indeterminate spaces and strange glowing colors produce a dream-like, hallucinatory effect. These figures have a dematerialized, ghostly quality to which the atom-like graininess of the image strongly contributes: a hand reaching out seems composed of glowing ectoplasm, a flattened mask-like face floats bodiless in a dark void.

The second group of images, the collages from two-dimensional materials, are no less ghostly. Many of these have been created from X-rays or negatives. There is a peculiar poignancy about the further dematerialization of these transparent images of the body's skeleton, negatives of once-fashionable clothes and old family snapshots. Positive photographic images are poetically or ironically juxtaposed: the confrontation of an old photograph of a locomotive wreck and an optimistically smiling girl of dated beauty (no. 48, plate XVI).

Many of Linda Connor's photographs relate to the twentieth century college and assemblage tradition in which the artist finds or selects objects and places them in new expressive contexts. In *High School Prom Commemorative* (no. 50, plate VII) souvenirs of past events are presented like votive objects. Their isolation on a dark, indeterminate background and the sharp-focus intensity of the print heighten our sense of the importance of the objects. In *Ethel* (no. 51) an inscribed high school graduation picture from the thirties has been mysteriously mutilated by the cutting away of Ethel's face. We are tantalized with suggestions of a history of personal relationships that we cannot know. This image is only one of a great many variations on the idea of the photograph within the photograph to be found in recent American photography.

Many of Linda Connor's images represent her personal vision of the natural world. In *Medical Chart with Leaves and Flowers* (no. 61) various small objects (leaves, flowers, shells, a broken doll, a tiny snapshot) are arranged upon a large-scale anatomical chart diagramming human reproduction. Partial hand coloring blurs distinctions between the "real" objects placed on the chart and the printed forms. The coloring appropriately suggests hand-colored natural history illustrations. A sense of the natural processes of birth, growth, and death is heightened by the leaf shadows that seem to drift across the image. In the works thus far discussed an almost miniaturistic scale is an important part of the intimate experience of examining the original print.

In some recent larger-scale works, objects are transformed by the use of a soft-focus lens. Linda Connor recently inherited from a great-aunt who had studied with the Pictorialist photographer Clarence White (1871–1925) a view camera with soft-focus lens. With this camera she has created such images as a leaf that swims in shimmering light (no. 55, plate XX), or two sprouting potatoes that might be phosphorescent sea creatures (no. 54). The poetry of

David Batchelder

Leslie Krims

these images is enhanced by chemical toning of the print, producing in this instance rich purple-browns.

Linda Connor does not always rearrange reality for the camera: she sometimes discovers a corner of the real world that fits perfectly into her vocabulary without the necessity for radical transformation. Such an image is the ceiling of Grand Central Station (no. 53) with its figures of personified constellations studded with light bulb stars.

Many of David Batchelder's photographs reveal a preoccupation with death and transience. The small nude figure of young Tristin is ringed by darkness (no. 63, plate XXI). A towel still holds the faint imprint of a vanished body (no. 64).

Batchelder is not only preoccupied with death: he often finds a strange beauty in it. His photographs of mummies (nos. 66, 67, plate XXII) have a shocking gothic impact; they are also sinuously graphic, even ornamental. It is not surprising that many of these images of death and mortality were made in Mexico, the land of the Day of the Dead and sugar candy skulls.

A number of images represent dead or dying animals. The partially plucked *Dead Quail* (no. 68, plate XXIII) hangs, not by its feet like birds in painted game pieces of the seventeenth or nineteenth centuries, but suspended in such a way as to suggest a crucified figure. The image of the mask-like antlered *Skull* (no. 69) was produced by means of a double exposure in the camera. The skull was first shot in close-up and then the camera refocused and the landscape recorded. The superimposition of the two shots on the same negative created the mist that enshrouds the landscape. Another image created by the same procedures is the mushroom (no. 70, plate XXIV). The spreading wings of the mushroom's cap and the slender stalk are an image of the awakening of new life, however fragile and translucent.

Leslie Krims' images range from the perverse and cruel to the magical. Although he has, on occasion, taken on documentary projects (his published portfolio, *The Deerslayers*, for example), all of the images seen here are set-ups that he has staged for his camera.

Humor, often tinged with cruelty, is very important to Krims' work: the slapstick blasphemy of the nude woman in Minnie Mouse mask striking a pose in front of a cross composed of mouse balloons (no. 74) or the original "photographic nude," a deadpan nude woman decorated with miniature cameras (no. 81). Some of Krims' imagery reminds one of the "black" humorists of recent American literature, such as Bruce Jay Friedman in his novel *A Mother's Kisses*: Mom, nude, covered with photographs of her son Les (no. 79) or the very literal illustration of the superstitious rhyme "step on a crack and break your mother's back" (no. 80).

Some images are not so much wickedly amusing as horrifying: the frightening gothic image of the screaming legless black man on a pedestal (no. 75, plate XXV) or the sequined spike heel impaling a white rat, an image which seems to embody the toughness, glitter, and indifference of the modern city (no. 76).

Krims is, however, capable on occasion of a quieter mood, as in the image (no. 85, plate XXVIII) in which a nude young woman leans over to whisper in the ear of an old woman seated in a chair on the lawn. Is the young woman a wood nymph, a messenger of Death, or are we witnessing an exchange of views between the ages? The mystery of this image is equalled by the charm of the photograph in which we are witness to an impromptu circus act in a living room (no. 83).

Many of Krims' photographs function metaphorically. The image of a nude woman in a domestic interior bearing on her back an enormous wedding cake (no. 78, plate XXVII) can be interpreted as an image of woman's enslavement by marriage bonds. In a similar fashion the image of the masked pregnant woman making a giant bubble can be seen as a metaphor for giving birth. The bubble resembles an enormous amnionic sac.

Judy Dater

The qualities of Krims' prints contribute greatly to the effect of his images. They are usually small in scale so that the staged scenes with their dark borders resemble miniature peep or shadow boxes. The brown tone of the image, the graininess, and the opaque shadows produce a graphic effect that removes the image from the immediacy of photographic reality. The use of a wide-angle lens and of flash illumination often serves to heighten the unreality of the scene recorded.

Judy Dater's photographs record the mysteries of human personality. Selecting her sitters from the floating population of San Francisco's Bohemia, she photographs them in their own, often fantastic, costumes. Sometimes she suggests a costume that she has seen the sitter wearing before or the sitters may spread out their wardrobe for the photographer's selection. The people are often exotic, the poses carefully contrived, but the photographic procedures are for the most part traditional, classic. Judy Dater's prints with their intensity of detail and richness of tone continue the West Coast tradition of Edward Weston and Imogen Cunningham.

These portraits stimulate thoughts about human diversity, about costume as self-expression, about role-playing. They also raise the question of to what degree the photographic portrait is a record of the sitter's personality or a projection of the photographer's fantasy. For this reason it is interesting to have in the exhibition two portraits of the same sitter, Kathleen Kelly; one formally posed, sharply recorded, almost a high fashion picture (no. 88), the second, with the baby China, full of mystery, transformed by the play of light and the blur of motion (no. 89, plate XXIX).

Light as an integral part of the image is most strikingly illustrated by the portrait of *Gwen* (no. 98). Here a sense of unease is created not only by the sitter's staring expression and the odd angle of her head but also by the blade of light that threatens to sever her head from her neck.

The role that costume plays in the communication of human personality is perhaps most strikingly seen in the portrait of *Suzan* (no. 97, plate XXXII), in which the sitter's vapid smile, her clown-like mask of make-up, and the identity of pattern between her dress and the chair she is seated in make one see her as an object rather than as a person. The images of the suited *Laura Mae* (no. 91, plate XXX) and the bespangled *Aarmour Starr* (no. 92, plate XXXI) further explore the relationship between costume and personality.

A number of the images in the exhibition, including the two just referred to, comment with gentle irony on questions of sexual identity and traditional sexual attitudes. *Cherie* (no. 95), a nude woman whose expression implies that she "has lived," holds in front of her a long framed photograph of an army company of World War I vintage. The image would simply be an amusingly literal illustration of an old-fashioned dirty joke were it not for the fact that this is also a strikingly direct portrait of an individual rather than of an anonymous model.

Benno Friedman

Kelly Wise

The majority of Friedman's works exhibited here are landscapes. Since the early sixteenth century, the making of landscape pictures has been the vehicle, not just for accurate topographical recording of the appearance of a particular place, but even more frequently for personal poetic expression: landscapes of the mind. Friedman's landscapes are part of this latter tradition: a boot of uncertain size is about to descend on a barren landscape, eroded desert landscapes glow with unexpected colors, an alien square of sky replaces one that has vanished (no. 104, plate XXXVI), an upright stone is surrounded by a mysterious flame-like halo.

Friedman is interested in painterly transformation of the photographic print. Although single or multiple negatives may be employed to create the image, the hand manipulation of each individual print results in unique works rather than repeatable images. The photographic image may be partially dissolved or bleached away, it may be subtly colored by chemical toning agents or dyes, or it may be colored by hand with a variety of materials. These painterly alterations give the images a dream-like fluidity: they melt and flow. There is also a considerable variety in the choice of printing papers: Friedman often chooses a paper with a strong grain or pebble pattern. While they may originally have been black and white, all of the images included in the exhibition are to one degree or another color images.

Kelly Wise's photographs deal with family relationships and the experience of living. His principal models are his own family, including the photographer himself. A young girl solemnly presses her breasts that are yet to be (no. 113, plate XXXIX). A wraith-like couple, blurs of motion in time, celebrate their anniversary beside a folding lounge chair that is slowly unraveling. Ironically, the chair is more sharply focused, more permanent and fixed than the ghostly human figures. An old man lies face down, resigned, on a pier that seems to lift into the sky (no. 116, plate XXXX).

The poetic or metaphorical sequential arrangement of photographic images is a very important part of this photographer's work. The photographic sequence "Early Morning" (nos. 118—123) is not a narrative in time but rather a poem about family life, human growth, and sexual roles. In this sequence light is as active a protagonist as the family members themselves. This may be clearly seen in the image of the *Child of Light* (no. 121), in which the figure of the striding young boy seems composed solely of the ever-changing elements of light and shadow.

Plates

All reproductions are actual size unless otherwise
indicated.
A complete listing of the works in the exhibition
will be found at the back of the book.

Emmet Gowin

Born 1941 in Danville, West Virginia;
currently living in Newtown, Pennsylvania,
and teaching at Princeton University.

Background

Richmond Professional Institute, Richmond,
Virginia, B.F.A., 1965.
Rhode Island School of Design, Providence,
M.F.A., 1967.
Studied with Harry Callahan.

Selected Exhibitions

Group

1969
George Eastman House, Rochester.
1970
"12 x 12," Carr House Gallery, Rhode Island
School of Design, Providence.
1971
George Eastman House, Rochester.
"Contemporary Photographers," Fogg Museum,
Harvard University.
1972
Museum of Modern Art, New York.
1974
"Celebrations," Hayden Gallery, Massachusetts
Institute of Technology, Cambridge.

One Man

1968
Dayton Art Institute, Dayton, Ohio.
1971
Creative Photography Gallery, Massachusetts
Institute of Technology, Cambridge.
The Photographer's Gallery, London.
1972
Light Gallery, New York.
1973
Friends of Photography at Carmel, California.
Light Gallery, New York.

Major Publications and References

1970
12 x 12 (exhibition catalogue), Providence,
R.I.: Rhode Island School of Design, 1970.
Be-ing without Clothes (exhibition catalogue),
Millerton, N.Y.: Aperture, 1970.
Album No. 5 (London), Summer, 1970.
Album No. 6 (London), Fall, 1970.
1971
The Art of Photography, Time-Life Library
of Photography, New York: Time-Life, 1971.
1972
Aperture, 16:3, 1972.
Art in Virginia, Richmond, Va.: Virginia
Museum of Fine Arts, 1972.
Camera Mainichi (Tokyo), October 1972.
Coleman, A. D. "Photography," *New York
Times*, 11 March 1972.
Photographing Children, Time-Life Library
of Photography, New York: Time-Life, 1972.
Thornton, Gene. "Photography," *New York
Times*, 9 January 1972.

1974
Celebrations (exhibition catalogue), Millerton,
N.Y.: Aperture, 1974.

Public Collections

Art Institute of Chicago
Cincinnati Art Museum
Dayton Art Institute
Fogg Museum, Harvard University
Minneapolis Institute of Arts
Museum of Art, Rhode Island School of Design,
Providence
The Library, Rhode Island School of Design,
Providence
University of Kansas Museum of Art, Lawrence

Plate I
EMMET GOWIN
Isle of Skye, 1972
(reduced)

Plate IV
EMMET GOWIN
Edith with Wild Berry Necklace
Danville, Virginia, 1971
(reduced)

Cary Wasserman

Born 1939 in Los Angeles; currently living in Cambridge, Massachusetts, while teaching and freelancing.

Background

University of California, Los Angeles, B.A., 1961.
University of California, Los Angeles, M.A., 1963.
Studied under Henry Holmes Smith.
Photographic study at the University of Indiana, Bloomington, 1967—70.
Photography critic, *Boston Globe*, 1970—73.
Art critic, *Boston Globe*, 1972.
Teacher of color photography and experimental processes, Art Institute, Boston, 1971—currently.

Selected Exhibitions

Group

1972
"Points of View," Institute of Contemporary Art, Boston.
"Food Art," Institute of Contemporary Art, Boston.
1973
"Faculty Show," Art Institute of Boston.

One Man

1968—70
University of Indiana, Bloomington.
1970
"Mexican Photographs," Polaroid Gallery, Cambridge.
Project, Inc., Cambridge.
1971
"Recent Photographs," Polaroid Gallery, Cambridge.
1972
Addison Gallery of American Art, Phillips Academy, Andover, Massachusetts.

Major Publications and References

1971
Goell, Jonathan. "Photography," *Boston Globe*, 7 November 1971.
Meatball (cover photograph), Berkeley, Calif.: Joel Deutsch, 1971.
1972
Goell, Jonathan. "Photography," *Boston Globe*, 18 January 1972.
Venture (Suffolk University [Boston] literary magazine), Winter, 1972. pp. 8, 19.

Plate V
CARY WASSERMAN
Tomb (Mary Baker Eddy), 1973
(original in color)

Jerry N. Uelsmann

Born 1934 in Detroit;
currently living in Gainesville, Florida,
and teaching at the University of Florida.

Background

Rochester Institute of Technology, Rochester,
New York, B.F.A., 1958.
Indiana University, Bloomington, M.S., M.F.A.,
1960.
Studied with Ralph Hattersley, Minor White,
and Henry Holmes Smith.
Founding member of the Society for Photo-
graphic Education, 1962.
Recipient of a Guggenheim Fellowship for
"Experiments in Multiple Printing Techniques
in Photography," 1967.
Delivered the fourth Bertram Cox Memorial
Lecture for the Royal Photographic Society
in London, 1971.

Selected Exhibitions

Group

1959
"Photography at Mid-Century," George Eastman
House, Rochester.
1965
"Photography in America 1850—1965," Yale
University Art Gallery.
1967
"Persistence of Vision," George Eastman House,
Rochester.
1968
"Photography as Printmaking," Museum of
Modern Art, New York.
1970
"Light ^{7}," Hayden Gallery, Massachusetts
Institute of Technology, Cambridge.
"12 x 12," Carr House Gallery, Rhode Island
School of Design, Providence.
1973
"Four Directions in Modern Photography,"
Yale University Art Gallery.
"Extraordinary Realities," Whitney Museum
of American Art, New York.

One Man

1960
Indiana University, Bloomington.
1966
Pratt Institute, New York.
1967
Museum of Modern Art, New York.
1968
Creative Photography Gallery, Massachusetts
Institute of Technology, Cambridge.
1969
Carl Siembab Gallery of Photography, Boston.
1972
Witkin Gallery, New York.

Major Publications and References

1959
Photography at Mid-Century (exhibition cata-
logue), Rochester, N.Y.: George Eastman
House, 1959.
1965
Photography in America 1850—1965 (exhibi-
tion catalogue), New Haven, Conn.: Yale
University Art Gallery, 1965.
1968
Light ^{7} (exhibition catalogue), Millerton, N.Y.:
Aperture, 1968.
1970
12 x 12 (exhibition catalogue), Providence,
R.I.: Rhode Island School of Design, 1970.
Bunnell, Peter C. *Jerry N. Uelsmann*, Millerton,
N.Y.: Aperture, 1970 (with bibliography).
Eight Photographs (portfolio), New York:
Doubleday, 1970. Introduction by William E.
Parker.
Ward, John L. *The Criticism of Photography
as Art: The Photographs of Jerry N. Uelsmann*,
Gainesville: University of Florida Press, 1970.
1972
Coleman, A. D. "Photography," *New York
Times*, 2 April 1972.
1973
Brettell, Richard. *Four Directions in Modern
Photography*, New Haven, Conn.: Yale Uni-
versity Art Gallery, 1973.
Doty, Robert, and Gorey, Edward. *Extra-
ordinary Realities* (exhibition catalogue), New
York: Whitney Museum of American Art, 1973.

Public Collections

Art Institute of Chicago
Birmingham Museum of Art, Birmingham,
Alabama
Detroit Institute of Arts
Florida Center for the Arts, University of
South Florida, Tampa
Fogg Art Museum, Harvard University
John and Mable Ringling Museum of Art,
Sarasota, Florida
Library of Congress, Washington, D.C.
Minneapolis Institute of Arts
Museum of Art, Rhode Island School of
Design, Providence
Museum of Modern Art, New York
Pasadena Museum of Modern Art, Pasadena,
California
Photographic Archives, University of Louis-
ville, Kentucky
Photographic Department, University of
California, Los Angeles
Sheldon Gallery, University of Nebraska,
Lincoln
Smithsonian Institution, Washington, D.C.
University Art Collection, Arizona State
University, Temple
University Art Gallery, University of Alabama,
Tuscaloosa
University Art Museum, University of New
Mexico, Albuquerque
University Museum, Southern Illinois Uni-
versity, Carbondale
University of Florida, Gainesville
University of Kansas Museum of Art,
Lawrence

Plate IX
JERRY UELSMANN
Untitled, 1971
(reduced)

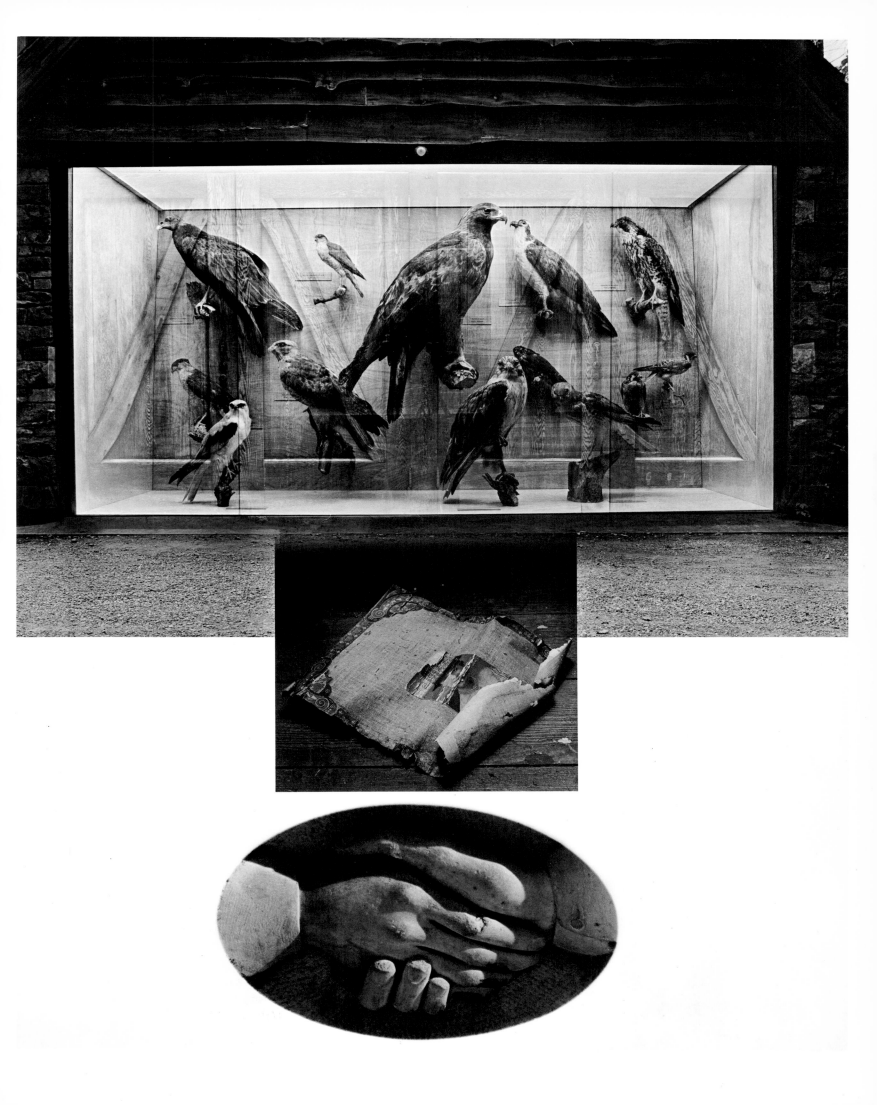

John Benson

Born 1927 in Sarasota, Florida; currently living in Philadelphia and teaching at the Moore College of Art in Philadelphia

Background

University of Georgia, Athens, B.A., 1950. University of Michigan, Ann Arbor, M.A., 1951. Studied with Minor White, 1964—65. Participated in graduate photography seminars with Harry Callahan at the Rhode Island School of Design, Providence, 1965—70.

Selected Exhibitions

Group

1968
Rhode Island School of Design, Providence.
1969
"Portrait Photographs," Museum of Modern Art, New York.
1970
"Be-ing without Clothes," Hayden Gallery, Massachusetts Institute of Technology, Cambridge.
1972
"The Expanded Photograph," Philadelphia Civic Center Museum.
1973
"Artist's Books," Moore College of Art, Philadelphia.
"Photographs from the Polaroid Collection," Museum of Fine Arts, Boston / Clarence Kennedy Gallery, Polaroid Corporation, Cambridge.

One Man

1968
Polaroid Gallery, Cambridge.
Carr House Gallery, Rhode Island School of Design, Providence.
1969
Addison Gallery of American Art, Phillips Academy, Andover, Massachusetts.
1970
Carr House Gallery, Rhode Island School of Design, Providence.
1973
Gerry Mansion, Rhode Island School of Design, Providence.

Major Publications and References

1968
Boston Review of Photography No. 5, March 1968, Cambridge, Mass.: Stephan G. Perrin.
Aperture 12:4, 1968.
1969
Portrait Photographs (exhibition catalogue), New York: Museum of Modern Art, 1969.
1970
Be-ing without Clothes (exhibition catalogue), Millerton, N.Y.: Aperture, 1970.
The Great Themes, Time-Life Library of Photography, New York: Time-Life, 1970.
1971
Camera, December 1971 (Lucerne: Bucher, Ltd.).
1972
The Expanded Photograph (exhibition catalogue), Philadelphia: Philadelphia Civic Center Museum, 1972.
1973
Artist's Books (exhibition catalogue), Philadelphia: Moore College of Art, 1973.

Public Collections

Art Institute of Chicago
Museum of Fine Arts, Boston
The Library, Rhode Island School of Design, Providence
Polaroid Corporation, Cambridge

Plate XIII
JOHN BENSON
Untitled, 1973
(reduced)

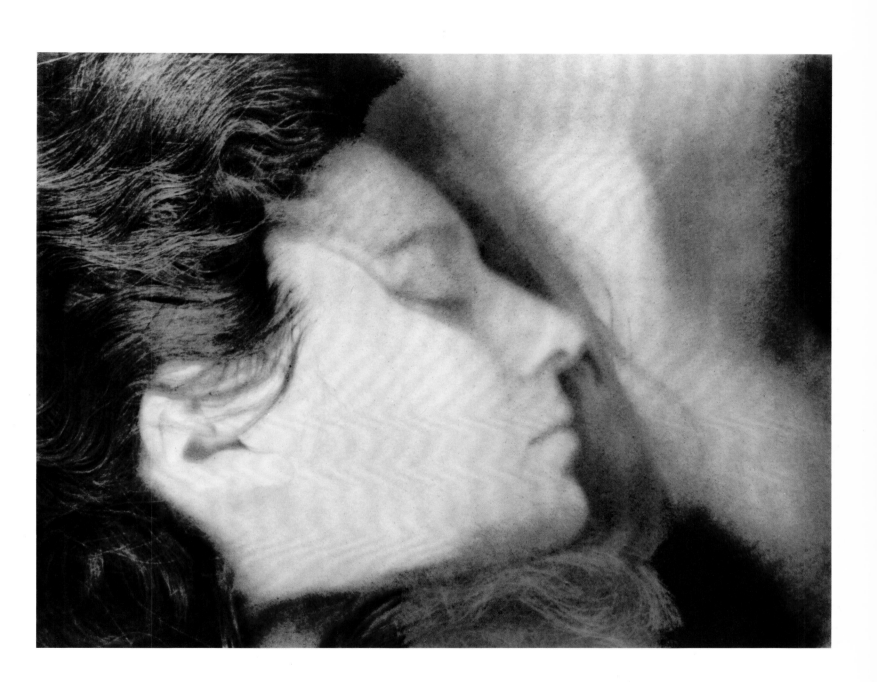

Plate XV
JOHN BENSON
Untitled, 1973
(original in color; reduced)

Plate XVI
JOHN BENSON
Untitled, 1973
(original in color; reduced)

Linda Connor

Born 1944 in New York City; currently living and teaching in San Francisco.

Background
Rhode Island School of Design, Providence, B.F.A., 1967.
Institute of Design, Illinois Institute of Technology, Chicago, M.S., 1969.
Studied with Harry Callahan, Aaron Siskind, and Arthur Siegel.

Selected Exhibitions

Group

1968
"Vision and Expression," George Eastman House, Rochester.

1970
"California Photographers," University of California at Davis.
"12 x 12," Carr House Gallery, Rhode Island School of Design, Providence.
"Be-ing without Clothes," Hayden Gallery, Massachusetts Institute of Technology, Cambridge.

1971
"Figure in Landscape," George Eastman House, Rochester.
"La Provençale," (invitation), Musée d'Arles, France.

1972
"Photographer as Magician," University of California at Davis.
"The Visual Dialogue Foundation, at the Friends of Photography, Carmel, California.

1973
"Imogen Cunningham — Linda Connor — Judy Dater," Musée Réattu, Arles, France.
"Light and Lens," Hudson River Museum, Yonkers, New York.
"Photographs from the Polaroid Collection," Museum of Fine Arts, Boston / Clarence Kennedy Gallery, Polaroid Corporation, Cambridge.

One Woman

1969
Photography Department, Dayton Art Institute, Dayton, Ohio.

1971
Photography Department, School of the Art Institute of Chicago.
San Francisco Art Institute.

1973
Light Gallery, New York.

Major Publications and References

1968
Vision and Expression (exhibition catalogue), Rochester, N.Y.: George Eastman House, 1968.

1970
California Photographers (exhibition catalogue), Davis, Calif.: University of California, 1970.
Photography Annual 1970 (New York), 1970.
12 x 12 (exhibition catalogue), Providence, R.I.: Rhode Island School of Design, 1970.
Be-ing without Clothes (exhibition catalogue), Millerton, N.Y.: Aperture, 1970.

1971
Creative Camera, March 1971 (London: Colin Osman).
Visual Dialogue Foundation (exhibition catalogue), Carmel, Calif.: Visual Dialogue Foundation and the Friends of Photography, 1972.

1973
Light and Lens (exhibition catalogue), Yonkers, N.Y.: Hudson River Museum, 1973.

Public Collections
Art Institute of Chicago
George Eastman House, Rochester
Musée d'Arles, France
National Gallery of Canada, Ottawa
Polaroid Collection, Cambridge
Ryerson Polytechnical Institute, Chicago
Virginia Museum of Fine Arts, Richmond
Yale University Art Gallery

Plate XVII
LINDA CONNOR
High School Prom Commemorative, 1972

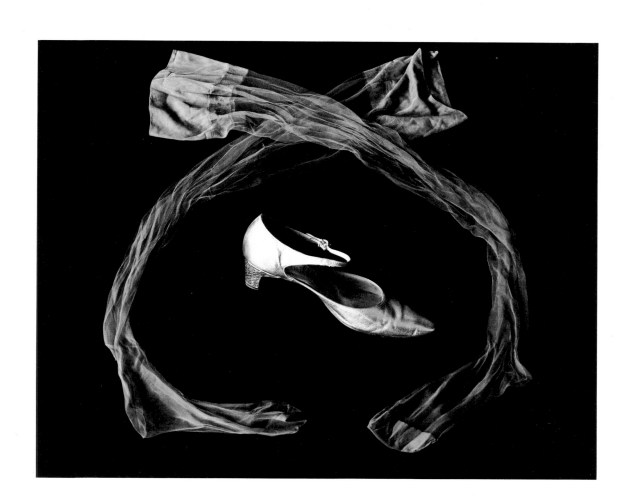

Plate XIX
LINDA CONNOR
Airplane, 1973
(reduced)

Plate XX
LINDA CONNOR
Leaf, 1973
(reduced)

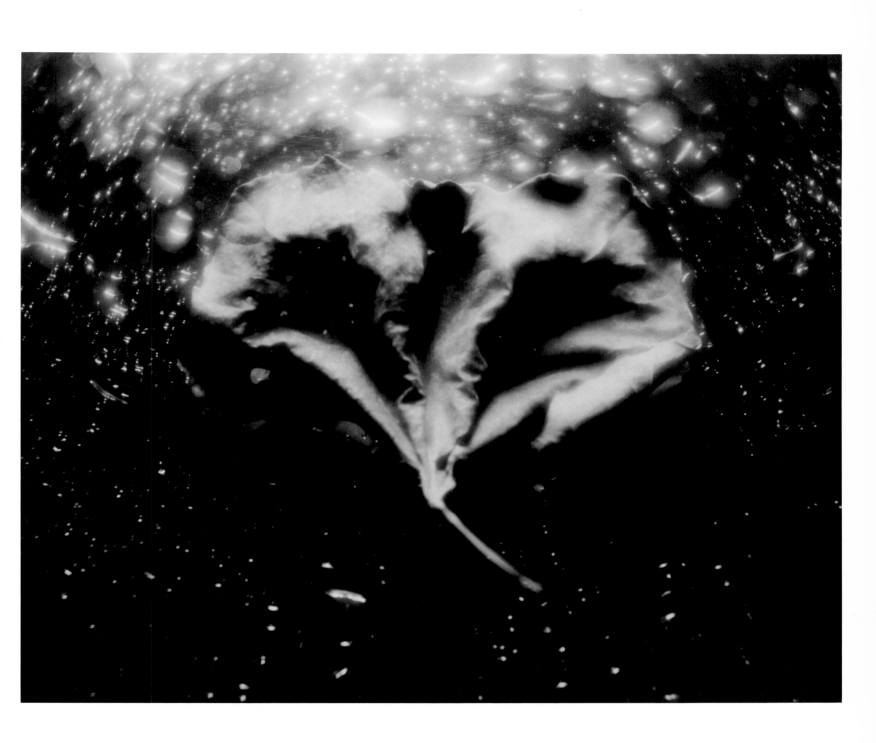

David Batchelder

Born 1939 in Titusville, Pennsylvania; currently living and teaching in Northampton, Massachusetts.

Background

University of New Hampshire, B.A., 1965.
University of Iowa, M.A., 1968.
Has served apprenticeships in medical and magazine photography.
Teaching assistant in photography at the University of Iowa.
Ford Foundation Grant to work on films, 1969.
Churchill Fund (Smith College) Grant to photograph in the West, 1971.

Selected Exhibitions

Group

1968
"Vision and Expression," George Eastman House, Rochester
"Light ^{7}," Hayden Gallery, Massachusetts Institute of Technology, Cambridge.
1970
"Be-ing without Clothes," Hayden Gallery, Massachusetts Institute of Technology, Cambridge.
1972
"Photovision 72," Institute of Contemporary Art, Boston
1973
Fogg Art Museum, Harvard University

One Man

1968
Bowdoin College, Brunswick, Maine.
1969
Exposure Gallery, New York.
1973
Addison Gallery of American Art, Phillips Academy, Andover, Massachusetts.

Major Publications and References

1968
Light ^{7} (exhibition catalogue), Millerton, N.Y.: Aperture, 1969.
Vision and Expression (exhibition catalogue), Rochester, N.Y.: George Eastman House, 1968.
1970
Augustus St. Gaudens: The Portrait Reliefs. New York: Grossmans, 1970. (photographs of sculpture by David Batchelder)
Be-ing without Clothes (exhibition catalogue), New York: Aperture, 1970.

Public Collections

Addison Gallery of American Art, Phillips Academy, Andover, Massachusetts
Bowdoin College, Brunswick, Maine
Fogg Museum, Harvard University
George Eastman House, Rochester
Massachusetts Institute of Technology, Cambridge
Smith College, Northampton, Massachusetts

Plate XXI
DAVID BATCHELDER
Tristin, 1968

Plate XXII
DAVID BATCHELDER
Mexico, 1970

Plate XXIII
DAVID BATCHELDER
Dead Quail, 1967
(reduced)

Leslie Krims

Born 1943 in New York City; currently living in Buffalo, New York, and teaching at the College of the State University of New York, Buffalo.

Background
Cooper Union, New York City, B.F.A., 1964.
Pratt Institute, New York City, M.F.A., 1967.
Assistant Instructor of Photography and Printmaking, Pratt Institute, 1966—67.
Teacher of photography, Rochester Institute of Technology, 1967—69.
National Education Association Fellowship, 1971, 1972.
New York State Council on the Arts Grant, 1971.

Selected Exhibitions

Group

1969
"Vision and Expression," George Eastman House, Rochester.
The Witkin Gallery, New York.
1970
"The Photograph as Object," National Gallery of Canada, Ottawa.
"12 x 12," Carr House Gallery, Rhode Island School of Design, Providence.
"Be-ing without Clothes," Hayden Gallery, Massachusetts Institute of Technology, Cambridge.
1972
"The Expanded Photograph," Philadelphia Civic Center Museum.
"Photographer as Magician," Memorial Union Art Gallery, University of California at Davis.
1973
"Art 4 '73," Internationale Kunstmesse, Basel.
"Critics Choice," Neikrug Gallery, New York.

One Man

1966
Pratt Institute, Brooklyn.
1969
Focus Gallery, San Francisco.
George Eastman House, Rochester.
Akron Art Institute, Akron, Ohio.
1970
Il Diaframma Gallery, Milan, Italy.
"Fictions," Galerie Prisma IV, Lund, Sweden.

1971
George Eastman House, Rochester.
Moore College, Philadelphia.
University of Colorado, Boulder.
The Toronto Gallery of Photography, Toronto.
1972
Album Fotogalerie, Cologne, West Germany.
The International Cultural Center, Antwerp, Belgium.
1973
Boston University, Boston.

Major Publications and References

1967
Aperture 13:3, 1967.
1969
Vision and Expression (exhibition catalogue), Rochester, N.Y.: George Eastman House, 1969.
1970
Album No. 4 (London), Spring, 1970.
Album No. 5 (London), Summer, 1970.
Album No. 6 (London), Fall, 1970.
Be-ing without Clothes (exhibition catalogue), Millerton, N.Y.: Aperture, 1970.
Camera, December 1970 (Lucerne: Bucher, Ltd.).
Camera Mainichi (Tokyo), August 1970.
Eight Photographs (portfolio), New York: Doubleday, 1970.
The Great Themes, Time-Life Library of Photography, New York: Time-Life, 1970.
1971
The Art of Photography. Time-Life Library of Photography, New York: Time-Life, 1971.
1972
Camera, February 1972 (Lucerne: Bucher, Ltd.).
Coleman, A. D. "Photography," *New York Times*, 12 March 1972.
The Deerslayers (portfolio), Buffalo, N.Y.: Les Krims, 1972.
The Little People of America (portfolio), Buffalo, N.Y.: Les Krims, 1972.
The Incredible Stack O' Wheat Murders (portfolio), Buffalo, N.Y.: Les Krims, 1972.
Making Chicken Soup (portfolio), Buffalo, N.Y.: Les Krims, 1972.
Thornton, Gene. "Photography," *New York Times*, 9 March 1972.
Shirey, D. L. "Photography," *New York Times*, 2 July 1972.

1973
Photography Year 1973. New York: Time-Life, 1973.

Public Collections
Art Museum, Rhode Island School of Design, Providence
George Eastman House, Rochester
Minneapolis Institute of the Arts, Minneapolis
Museum of Modern Art, New York
National Gallery of Canada, Ottawa
Ohio Wesleyan University, Delaware, Ohio
State University of New York, Genesco
University of Kansas Art Museum, Lawrence
University of New Mexico Museum of Art, Albuquerque

Plate XXV
LESLIE KRIMS
Untitled, 1970

Plate XXVI
LESLIE KRIMS
Untitled, 1968

Judy Dater

Born 1941 in Los Angeles; currently living and working in San Anselmo, California.

Background

Art School, University of California, Los Angeles, 1959—62.
San Francisco State College, B.A., 1963.
San Francisco State College, M.A., 1966.
Studied with Jack Welpott.

Selected Exhibitions

Group

1968

"Vision and Expression," George Eastman House, Rochester.
"Light [7]," Hayden Gallery, Massachusetts Institute of Technology, Cambridge.

1970

"Be-ing without Clothes," Hayden Gallery, Massachusetts Institute of Technology, Cambridge.
"California Photographers," Oakland Museum, Oakland, California.
The Witkin Gallery, New York.

1972

"Portfolios," Oakland Museum, Oakland.
Visual Dialogue Foundation at the Friends of Photography, Carmel, California.

1973

"Imogen Cunningham — Linda Connor — Judy Dater," Musée Réattu, Arles, France.
"Women, Judy Dater / Jack Welpott," George Eastman House, Rochester.

One Woman

1972

School of the Art Institute of Chicago.
Center for Photographic Studies, Louisville, Kentucky.
The Witkin Gallery, New York.

1973

University of Maryland School of Architecture, College Park.

Major Publications and References

1968

Vision and Expression (exhibition catalogue), Rochester, N.Y.: George Eastman House, 1968.
Light [7] (exhibition catalogue), Millerton, N.Y.: Aperture, 1968.

1970

Be-ing without Clothes (exhibition catalogue), Millerton, N.Y.: Aperture, 1970.
California Photographers (exhibition catalogue), Oakland, Calif.: Oakland Museum, 1970.

1972

Mellow, J. R. "Photography," *New York Times*, 27 May 1972.
Tucker, Anne. *Judy Dater: Sexual Women and Fearsome Landscape*, Rochester, N.Y.: Visual Studies Workshop, 1972.
Visual Dialogue Foundation (exhibition catalogue), Carmel, Calif.: Friends of Photography, 1972.

1973

North, Kenda S. *"Ms.": Subtle Discrepancies of Sexual Inference*, Rochester, N.Y.: Visual Studies Workshop, 1973.
Tucker, Anne. *The Woman's Eye*, New York: Knopf, 1973.

1974

Coleman, A. D. "Photography," *New York Times*, 13 January 1974.

Public Collections

Bibliothèque Nationale, Paris
Fogg Museum, Harvard University
George Eastman House, Rochester
Institute for Sex Research, Indiana University, Bloomington
Museum of Fine Arts, Boston
Museum of Modern Art, New York
Oakland Museum, Oakland, California
Pasadena Museum of Modern Art, Pasadena
San Francisco Museum of Art
University Art Museum, University of New Mexico, Albuquerque
University of Kansas Museum of Art, Lawrence
University of Maryland

Plate XXIX
JUDY DATER
Kathleen and China, 1972

Plate XXX
JUDY DATER
Laura Mae, 1973

Plate XXXI
JUDY DATER
Aarmour Starr, 1972

Benno Friedman

Born 1945 in New York City; currently living and working in Sheffield, Massachusetts, and New York City.

Background
Brandeis University, Waltham, Massachusetts, B.A., 1966.

Selected Exhibitions
Group
1970
"Boston Band," Parker 470, Boston.
"Be-ing without Clothes," Hayden Gallery, Massachusetts Institute of Technology, Cambridge.
1971
Light Gallery, New York.
1972
"60's Continuum," George Eastman House, Rochester.
"Points of View," Institute of Contemporary Art, Boston
"Octave of Prayer," Hayden Gallery, Massachusetts Institute of Technology, Cambridge.
"Photovision 72," Boston Center for the Arts.
1973
"Light and Lens," Hudson River Museum, Yonkers, New York.

One Man

1969
Underground Gallery, New York City.
1970
Art Union, Lenox, Massachusetts.
1972
Addison Gallery of American Art, Phillips Academy, Andover, Massachusetts.
1973
Gallery of Modern Art, Tucson, Arizona.
Light Gallery, New York.

Major Publications and References
1970
Be-ing without Clothes (exhibition catalogue), Millerton, N.Y.: Aperture, 1970.
Art in America, March—April 1970, p. 100.
1972
Octave of Prayer (exhibition catalogue), Millerton, N.Y.: Aperture, 1972.
1973
Light and Lens (exhibition catalogue), Yonkers, N.Y.: Hudson River Museum, 1973.

Public Collections

Fogg Museum, Harvard University
Museum of Modern Art, New York

Plate XXXIII
BENNO FRIEDMAN
Untitled, 1972—73
(original in color)

Plate XXXIV
BENNO FRIEDMAN
Cheri Hiser, 1971
(original in color)

Plate XXXV
BENNO FRIEDMAN
Untitled, 1970
(original in color)

Plate XXXVI
BENNO FRIEDMAN
Untitled, 1972
from a series
(original in color)

Kelly Wise

Born 1932 in New Castle, Indiana; currently
on sabbatical from Phillips Academy, Andover,
Massachusetts, and living in Center Harbor,
New Hampshire.

Background
Purdue University, B.S.A., 1955.
Columbia University, New York, M.F.A., 1959.
Art Consultant in Art and English, National
Humanities Faculty, National Endowment
for the Humanities, 1973–74.

Selected Exhibitions

Group

1969
"Exhibition 2," Massachusetts Institute of
Technology, Cambridge.
1971
Addison Gallery of American Art, Phillips
Academy, Andover, Massachusetts.
1972
Institute of Contemporary Art, Boston.
"Octave of Prayer," Hayden Gallery,
Massachusetts Institute of Technology,
Cambridge.
"Self-Portraits," Zone V Gallery, Cambridge.
1973
Fogg Museum, Harvard University.

Major Publications and References

1972
Octave of Prayer (exhibition catalogue),
Millerton, N.Y.: Aperture, 1972.
1973
Points of View (exhibition catalogue in post-
card form; 1 image), Boston: Institute of
Contemporary Art, 1973.

Public Collections

Addison Gallery of American Art, Phillips
Academy, Andover, Massachusetts
Colorado Photographic Arts Center, Denver
Lawrence General Hospital, Lawrence,
Massachusetts

Plate XXXVII
KELLY WISE
Reflection, 1973

Plate XXXVIII
KELLY WISE
Stairway, 1972

Plate XXXIX
KELLY WISE
Child Rite, 1972

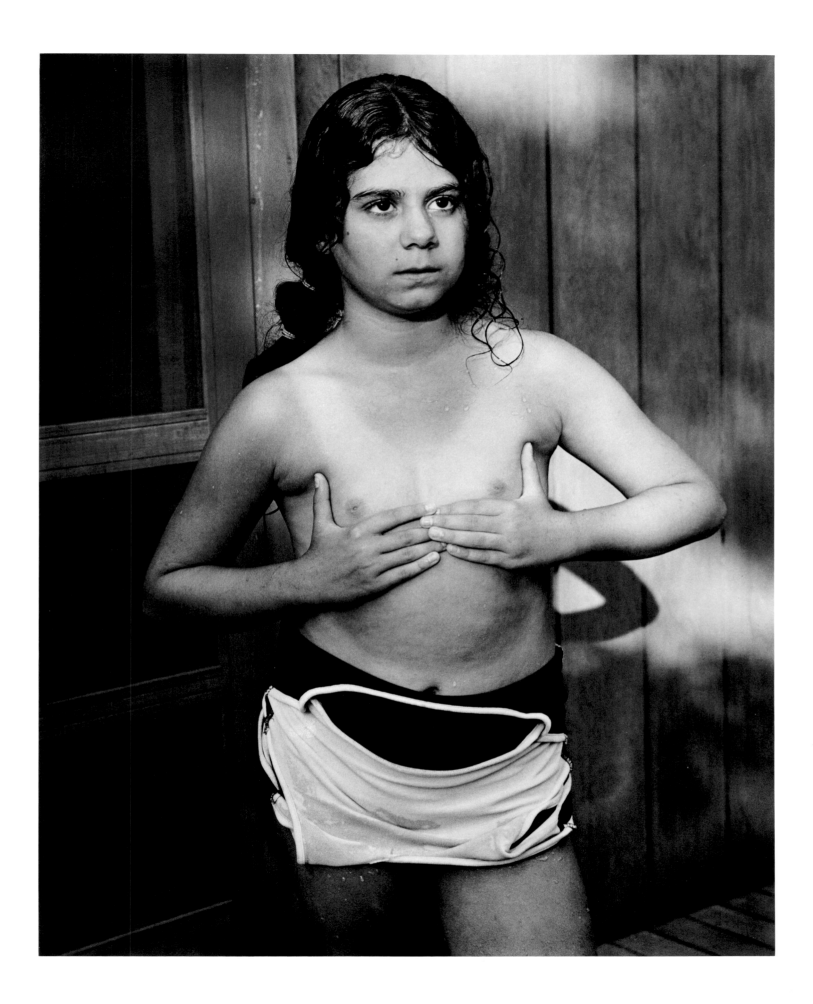

Plate XXXX
KELLY WISE
The Pier, 1973

Checklist

of the exhibition

All measurements are to the nearest 1/8 inch.
Height precedes width.
Asterisks denote works reproduced in this book.

Emmet Gowin

Lent by the photographer.

1
Earth Bank, Danville, Virginia, 1971
7½ x 9½ in.

2 *
Isle of Skye, 1972
7½ x 9½ in.

3
Sheep's Fleece, Yorkshire, England, 1972
7½ x 9½ in.

4
Dalton Dishman, Ice Carver, Dayton, Ohio,
1970
6 x 6 in.

5 *
Ice Fish, Danville, Virginia, 1971
7½ x 9½ in.

6 *
Nancy Wells (with eggs), Danville, Virginia,
1969
5¼ x 6½ in.

7
Edith and Rennie Booher, Danville, Virginia,
1969
5¼ x 6¾ in.

8
Elijah (on patchwork quilt), 1968
5 x 6½ in.

9
Nancy (with dolls), Danville, Virginia, 1965
5½ x 6¾ in.

10
Edith, Danville, Virginia, 1970
7½ x 9½ in.

11 *
Edith with Wild Berry Necklace, Danville,
Virginia, 1971
7½ x 9½ in.

12
Nancy Wells (twine and blanket construction),
Danville, Virginia, 1971
7½ x 9½ in.

Cary Wasserman

All prints are in color.
Lent by the photographer.

13 *
Tomb (Mary Baker Eddy), 1973
9¾ x 7½ in.

14 *
Priest and Christ, 1972
9 5/8 x 7 5/8 in.

15
Phillip and Apollo, 1972
10 x 12 7/8 in.

16
Trio, 1973
9½ x 7½ in.

17
Cozy Corner Café, 1973
7½ x 9 5/8 in.

18
Birthday Party, 1971
7 5/8 x 9¾ in.

19
Elysian Fields (ascent), 1973
7½ x 9 5/8 in.

20 *
Elysian Fields, 1973
7½ x 9 5/8 in.

21 *
Magnolia No. 1, Pink Rock, 1973
7½ x 9½ in.

22
Magnolia No. 2, Center on Blue, 1971
7½ x 9½ in.

23
Magnolia No. 3, Green Indentation, 1971
7½ x 9½ in.

24
Magnolia No. 4, Vertical Face, 1971
9¼ x 7¼ in.

Jerry Uelsmann

Lent by the photographer.

25
Untitled, 1972
11½ x 10½ in.

26 *
Untitled, 1971
13¼ x 10¼ in.

Diptych, 1972

27 *
Top half: *Rock Angel*, 1972
9 3/8 x 12 3/8 in.

28 *
Bottom half: *Untitled*, 1972
10½ x 12 3/8 in.

29 *
Untitled, 1969
9 7/8 x 12 3/8 in.

Triptych, 1972

30
Left: 1972
12½ x 10¼ in.

31
Center: 1972
11¾ x 9¼ in. (arched top)

32
Right: 1972
12½ x 10¼ in.

33
Untitled, 1972
12 x 9 in.

34
Navigation without Numbers, 1971
11¼ x 10¼ in.

35
Questioning Moment, 1971
10 5/8 x 13 5/8 in.

36 *
Untitled, 1973
12½ x 9 7/8 in.

37 *
Untitled, 1972
6½ x 9 in. (oval)

John Benson

All prints are laminated 3M color copier prints.
Lent by the photographer.

38 *
Untitled (yellow profile), 1973
8½ x 11 in.

39
Untitled (back of head), 1973
8½ x 11 in.

40 *
Untitled (heads, hand), 1973
8½ x 11 in.

41
Untitled (face), 1973
8½ x 11 in.

42

Untitled (face floating), 1973
8½ x 11 in.

43

Untitled (profile, lighted panel), 1973
11 x 8½ in.

44

Untitled (skull), 1973
11 x 8½ in.

45

Untitled (collage with x-ray), 1973
8½ x 11 in.

46

Untitled (dresses), 1973
8½ x 11 in.

47 *

Untitled (negative collage), 1973
8½ x 11 in.

48 *

Untitled (wreck), 1973
8½ x 11 in.

49

Untitled (ball team), 1973
8½ x 11 in.

Linda Connor

Number 12 is hand colored.
Lent by the photographer.

50 *

High School Prom Commemorative, 1972
4¾ x 6 in.

51

Ethel (1932), 1972
4 3/8 x 3 3/8 in.

52

Constellation, 1971
7 5/8 x 4¾ in.

53

Ceiling, Grand Central Station, 1973
6 7/8 x 4 5/8 in.

54

Potatoes, 1973
7½ x 9¼ in.

55 *

Leaf, 1973
7½ x 9¼ in.

56

Untitled (Golden Gate Park), 1972
7½ x 9¼ in.

57 *

Airplane, 1973
7½ x 9¼ in.

58

Untitled (bird on leaf), 1972
5¼ x 5½ in.

59 *

Dove, 1972
4¾ x 6¼ in.

60

One from a series of "Sea Creatures," 1971
6 x 4 5/8 in.

61

Medical Chart with Leaves and Flowers, 1970
6 1/8 x 4 5/8 in.

David Batchelder

Lent by the photographer.

62

Elaine Washing Dishes, New Hampshire, 1972
9½ x 9¾ in.

63 *

Tristin, 1968
6 1/8 x 9 1/8 in.

64

Towel, Mexico, 1970
9 1/8 x 6 1/8 in.

65

Photographs of Children Since Dead, Mexico, 1970
6 1/8 x 8 7/8 in.

66 *

Mexico (mummy), 1970
6 x 8 7/8 in.

67

Dead Woman, Mexico, 1970
12 7/8 x 9 5/8 in.

68 *

Dead Quail, 1967
10¾ x 7 1/8 in.

69

Skull, Utah, 1971
9¼ x 9 1/8 in.

70 *

Alexandria, New Hampshire (mushroom), 1972
9¾ x 9½ in.

71

Alexandria, New Hampshire (trees), 1973
9¾ x 9½ in.

72

Dying Pigeon, 1968
7 x 10½ in.

73

Mexico (shadow), 1970
6 x 9 in.

Leslie Krims

All are toned Kodalith prints.
Lent by the photographer.

74

Untitled (Minnie Mouse cross), 1968
4 5/8 x 6¾ in.

75 *

Untitled (legless man on pedestal), 1970
4 5/8 x 6¾ in.

76

Untitled (high heels and white rat), 1971
6 7/8 x 4¾ in.

77 *

Untitled (masked woman making bubble), 1968
4 5/8 x 6¾ in.

78 *

Untitled (woman supporting wedding cake on her back), 1971
4 5/8 x 6¾ in.

79

Untitled (mother with son's photographs), 1971
6¾ x 4½ in.

80

Untitled ("Step on a crack . . . "), 1971
6¾ x 4½ in.

81

Untitled (nude woman with cameras), 1972
4 5/8 x 6¾ in.

82

Untitled (outlined nude woman), 1972
4 5/8 x 6 7/8 in.

83

Untitled (circus act), 1972
4 5/8 x 6 7/8 in.

84

Untitled (magic trick), 1970
4 5/8 x 6¾ in.

85 *

Untitled (young woman whispering in old woman's ear), 1971
4 5/8 x 6¾ in.

Judy Dater

Lent by the photographer.

86

Lucia, 1972
9½ x 7½ in.

87

Twinka, 1970
9 3/8 x 7 3/8 in.

88
Kathleen Kelly, 1972
9¼ x 7¼ in.

89 *
Kathleen and China, 1972
9½ x 7 1/8 in.

90
Valerie van Cleve, 1972
9¼ x 7 1/8 in.

91 *
Laura Mae, 1973
9½ x 7½ in.

92 *
Aarmour Starr, 1972
9 3/8 x 7¼ in.

93
Tex, 1973
7½ x 9½ in.

94
Daydreams, 1973
7½ x 9½ in.

95
Cherie, 1972
7¼ x 9¼ in.

96
Maria Moreno, 1970
9½ x 7½ in.

97 *
Suzan , 1971
9 3/8 x 7 3/8 in.

98
Gwen, 1972
9¼ x 7¼ in.

Benno Friedman

Most of the prints have been altered by chemical bleaching and toning. Several are hand colored.
Lent by courtesy of the Light Gallery, New York.

99 *
Untitled (figures in train), 1972–73
6 x 7½ in.

100
Untitled (landscape with storage tank and woman's face), 1971, from a series
7 1/8 x 5 1/8 in.

101 *
Cheri Hiser, 1971
5½ x 5 7/8 in.

102
Untitled (two figures seen through tunnel of leaves), 1970
7 7/8 x 5 3/8 in.

103
Untitled (beach with palm), 1972
6 7/8 x 7 5/8 in.

104 *
Untitled (tree and square of sky), 1972, from a series
7 7/8 x 6 7/8 in.

105 *
Untitled (rock casting shadow), 1970
7 3/8 x 5¼ in.

106
Untitled (nude woman at edge of water), 1970–73
7 3/8 x 7 7/8 in.

107
Untitled (boot over landscape), 1970
5 x 6 5/8 in.

108
Untitled (luminous rock seen through grasses), 1970–73
8 7/8 x 6 in.

109
Untitled (eroded hill, pink sky), 1971
6 x 8 in.

110
Untitled (desert landscape, moon), 1971
5½ x 7½ in.

Kelly Wise

Lent by the photographer.

111 *
Reflection, 1973
10 x 8 in.

112 *
Stairway, 1972
10 1/8 x 7¾ in.

113 *
Child Rite, 1972
9¾ x 7¾ in.

114
Anniversary, 1973
9½ x 11¼ in.

115
Wayne Frederick, 1973
9¾ x 6¾ in.

116 *
The Pier, 1973
11 1/8 x 8 7/8 in.

117
Swing, 1972
8 x 10 in.

Sequence: "Early Morning," 1972–73
118
Mother, 1972
10¾ x 8½ in.

119
Morning Washes, 1972
8½ x 10¾ in.

120
Sink, 1972
8½ x 10¾ in.

121
Child of Light, 1972
8 3/8 x 10¾ in.

122
Father, 1973
10½ x 7 7/8 in.

123
Candle, 1973
8 3/8 x 10 7/8 in.